"So God Made A Farmer:"

A Retrospective on
The Living Words of Paul Harvey
by an Organic Farmer

Levi Lyle

ICE SAGE

So God Made A Farmer

Levi Lyle

Copyright ©2021 by Levi Lyle

First Edition.

Softcover ISBN: 978-1-4218-3692-8

Hardcover ISBN: 978-1-4218-3693-5

Library of Congress Control Number: 2021936502

All rights reserved. Printed in the United States of America. No part of this book may be used or reproduced in any manner whatsoever without written permission except in the case of brief quotations embodied in critical articles and reviews. For information contact:

1ST WORLD LIBRARY
PO Box 2211
Fairfield, Iowa 52556
www.1stworldpublishing.com

LEVI'S INDIGENOUS FRUIT ENTERPRISES
1045 210th St,
Keota, IA 52248
Levi@levilyle.com

Praise for *So God Made A Farmer*

"With farmers facing climate challenges now more than ever – we need bold leaders and innovative strategies to reshape U.S. food and farm policy. Lyle calls us to action to revitalize the American farm and revolutionize the future of farming in the U.S."

—Rosalyn Lehman, Executive Director, Iowa Organic Association

"Driven by an in depth understanding of natural systems and a thoughtfulness carved by intimate personal experience on the land, Lyle's own anecdotes as a farmer lights a hopeful path forward. He artfully applies the show don't tell principle here to make soil health and place-based philosophies more tangible."

—Christophe Jospe, President, Carbon A List

'This books shows a deep understanding of the land. Lyle's use of past and present examples form a well-honed perspective of the many intricacies of life as a farmer. His perceptions for the future brings some hope that land management will trend in a direction that is more favorable toward environmental stewardship.'

—Patrick O'Malley, Ph.D., Native Fruit Association

"Levi Lyle is not just a philosopher of the history and culture of agriculture; he is an innovative farmer who marries technology with ecology. This book will take you on a wistful journey through the changes that have brought us to today's agriculture, but pay close attention to the regenerative farming practices Levi sprinkles throughout the narrative. If adopted widely by both organic and conventional farmers, these practices will have wide-reaching benefits for our local environments and our planet: reducing soil erosion, improving water quality, sequestering carbon in soils, improving soil water-holding capacity and reducing flooding, and creating healthier and more diverse landscapes."

—Francis Thicke
Soil scientist and organic farmer,
Board member of the Real Organic Project

"Levi Lyle exposes the fundamental flaws in our system of modern, industrialized agriculture and uses personal anecdotes to illustrate the resulting high cost in suffering to its victims. He articulates a number of well-reasoned remedies to begin the process of changing course. Finally, he lays out a regenerative vision for the future of agriculture—or, as he put it--…correct our mistakes and make the path right…."

—Tom Wahl
Red Fern Farm

"In a state dominated by mono-cropped GMO corn and soybeans and hog factory farms, sixth generation farmer Levi Lyle offers a new, comprehensive, and holistic, yet practical vision to regenerate rural Iowa—and America—that he thoughtfully and eloquently presents in *"So God Made a Farmer:" A Retrospective on The Living Words of Paul Harvey by an Organic Farmer*.

Levi sees the problems with the current corporate dominated industrial agriculture methods that are eroding Iowa's rich soils, polluting its waterways, and hollowing out its once vibrant small towns. But Levi's thoughtful message is not one of division but one of hope, aiming to bring people together to revive rural communities. Levi's perspective is solidly grounded on his family farm with its diversified production based on organic and regenerative agriculture practices.

Levi Lyle is not only a farmer, but in his prolific writings, such as *So God Made a Farmer*, he is also an eloquent spokesperson for a new vision of agriculture that is quickly gaining ground in America and around the world. In this way, Levi Lyle may become the Wendell Berry of his generation."

—Ken Roseboro, editor, The Organic & Non-GMO Report

"Paul Harvey would be proud of Levi Lyle. He truly embodies what it means to be a steward of the land. He has shown that working with nature can not only improve the environment, but can be financially profitable as well. Just as aronia berries can rejuvenate your health, so too can his methods of farming rejuvenate the soil and preserve it for future generations."

—Dale Hilgenkamp, President
American Aronia Berry Association

Thank you Jill for your endearing love and support.

Acknowledgments

In this, the second book of five to be published in the Ice Sage Series, there is an ever-present cadence to the energy I devote to the project. It is a distinct phase of solving any problem to first fully understand the roads we have traveled. *"So God Made A Farmer:" A Retrospective on The Living Words of Paul Harvey by an Organic Farmer* draws lessons from missteps by our agricultural community and celebrates the unwavering strength of the rural ethic—both invaluable, will deliver us to a future magnificent to behold.

I would like to extend my gratitude to the following people: my wife, Jill, whose natural gift of patience I aspire to; my father, Trent, for lighting the way for me to farm; Margaret Wilson, as well as my mother, Joy, for editing; Werner Elmker for assisting with cover art; Wendell Berry, Wes Jackson, Ray Archuleta, John Fullerton, and the late Paul Harvey for their leadership and inspiration.

I am grateful to Connie Mutel for first publishing my incorporated essay titled "Regenerative Stewardship," in her book *Introduction to Iowa's Environmental Problems* (working title) and to the Iowa Poetry Association for first publishing my poem titled "Square Mile" in *Lyrical Iowa*.

Square Mile

By Levi Lyle, *Ice Sage: Living and Loving the Land Poems*

One family, two families, three families, more
640, 320, 160 acres divided by four
steward oats, corn, soybean, hay and
rotate- the families multiply and stay.

Consolidate the farms
mechanize the man
increase the acres
mine what ye' can.

Progress
4, 3, 2, 1
close down the school
the kids have all gone.

Table of Contents

Introduction xv
Chapter 1: Caretaking 1
Chapter 2: Commitment 5
Chapter 3: Neighborliness 15
Chapter 4: Resourcefulness 19
Chapter 5: Balance 26
Chapter 6: Stewardship 33
Chapter 7: Legacy 42
Conclusion 45
Appendix A 48
Appendix B 52

Introduction

Like many farm kids, after high school I left without a plan to return. More than ten years later, it was the arrival of children which gave new perspective to my wife and I. Family would become the guiding light, both the candle illuminating the way and the ever-present gravity around which all else revolves.

When opportunity to move back to the community where we both had been raised came, we knew it was the right decision. Both our families still resided on farms there. For a while I would maintain an off the farm job, but inspiration would pave the way toward full time farming and organic agriculture.

Previously, as a running back on the University of Northern Iowa (UNI) Football team, I had experienced valuable lessons in the power of food as medicine. My journey to achieve optimal performance, coupled with a diagnosis of cancer in my father, which he had successfully overcome, was at work within me. I knew I needed to align my farming practices with what I felt was right.

I was only five years old when my dad was diagnosed with stage four cancer. This was in the 80's when the agricultural pesticide DDT had impacted bald eagle populations and the species was on the brink of extinction. I had only rarely seen a bald eagle until I moved back to the farm in 2010 and found populations had recovered. Now they can be seen daily on the prairie and nesting high in old oak trees. To me, how we farm, the state of our environment, and the prevalence of cancer are threads of a single story about our rural communities.

The overwhelming issue of our time is the destruction of land and people.

While researching to write *"So God Made A Farmer:" A Retrospective on The Living Words of Paul Harvey by an Organic Farmer*, I came upon the widely viewed and controversial advertisement transposing Paul Harvey's honorable poem onto a commercial for Dodge Ram pickup trucks promoted during Super Bowl XLVII.

Harvey's poem was first read as part of his keynote speech at the 1978 Future Farmers of America National Convention. The Dodge commercial became controversial because it exploited the iconic images of rural America.

When large corporations, and the special interests representing them, use salt-of-the-Earth metaphors like the steadfastness of the rural farmer to promote their brand, to some it feels condescending and contradictory to the corruption and questionable ethics lurking behind their messaging.

The United States Department of Agriculture (USDA) National Agricultural Statistics Service and the Census of Agriculture tell the whole story. The data shows a decline of family farms exalted by Dodge. My home state of Iowa, by the day, has fewer farms, less diversity, more synthetic inputs, more polluted water, more soil loss, more habitat loss, and fast dwindling rural schools and community ties (see "A Changing Landscape").

> **A Changing Landscape**
> - In the U.S., the 273,000 smallest farms (less than ten acres) make up .1% of all farmland while the 85,127 largest farms (2,000 or more acres) make up 58% of farmland.
> - In the last 55 years, the number of Iowa farms has decreased by nearly 75%: 206,000 farms to just 89,000, while the number of acres farmed has remained steady.
> - Iowa used to be a leading producer of oats, apples, potatoes, cherries, wheat, and more. Today, Iowa farms predominantly raise corn, soybeans, and hogs.
> - Iowa is the nation's top pig producer. But profit per pig today is just over $6, a drastic decrease from the $111 per pig in 1976, a year after Harvey wrote his original version of "So God Made A Farmer" in The Gadsden Times newspaper.
>
> USDA National Agricultural Statistics Service, 2017.

There are barriers which discourage young farmers from entering agriculture: the high cost and limited access to farmland; start up investment in equipment and inputs; experience in farm management and the array of highly specialized skills; and the uncertainty and volatility of markets. Without support and encouragement from my father, who still is actively involved in the day-to-day operation, I would have had difficulty getting started.

Challenging But Not Impossible
In 1980, the U.S. Olympic Hockey team won gold. The fabled event "Miracle on Ice." was made into a movie called *Miracle*. In real life, the U.S. team was hailed as underdogs against a bigger, faster, stronger, and more experienced U.S.S.R. team, and rightly so. But as Vince Lombardi once said, "Life's battles don't always go to the stronger or faster man. But sooner or later, the man who wins is the man who thinks he can."

Lombardi was speaking, of course, about the element of sheer will in achievement and the great power in unifying behind a communal purpose. There are a thousand examples I could use, but I chose the 1980 Olympic Hockey team: first, because it's a patriotic story, and most farmers I know have a strong sense of patriotism about their reasons for farming. Farmers associate their pride in productivity and yield with patriotism for the USA. Secondly, the analogy of the '80 U.S. Olympic Hockey team offers an unexpected analogy to farming that I'll describe more in the final chapter.

Purpose + Will = Achievement of Goals
My first book, *Ice Sage: Living and Loving the Land Poems*, goes about this plan as described, building a foundation. I want to vitalize you, my loyal supportive team, as I unite rather than divide, with a message that bends toward hope.

Book two of the series, *Ice Sage: Living and Loving the Land*

Prose, soon to be published, is a memoir of the changes I've seen in agriculture during my lifetime. It is a call to action that we, each of us, must first know where we come from in order to know where we are going. Every rural community has a local culture maintained through the stories (and sometimes songs), knowledge, and experience of the local geography, and a multi-generational perspective of changes to both.

Ultimately, when the stories we tell are more often about what we've seen on television than what parents, grandparents and influential mentors have endowed to local memory, the depravity of our purpose, or otherwise laissez-faire consignation as stewards-of-nothing, grows ever more bankrupt.

My third book, *The Keota Protocol: Community Sponsored Agriculture to Renew Land, Culture, and Climate Crisis (working title)*, is where solutions arise. Learn how we will revolutionize our relationship to land, ecosystems, and planet (climate change included), and succeed by uniting.

You can think of *"So God Made A Farmer:" A Retrospective on The Living Words of Paul Harvey by an Organic Farmer* as an introduction to my upcoming works. I assure you these four books will make you laugh and cry (sometimes at the same time). Together, as conscientious, rational, and sincere citizens, our voice will speak resolutely as it offers solutions not for the future but for today.

I make a promise to my readers.
More than ever, we can agree on the need to unite liberal and conservative; Wall Street and Main Street; Black, White, Latino;

straight and LGBTQ+ communities. My energy will always be directed toward finding common ground to build relationships. Too often, we see people fueling an environment of coercion and dissention. Such people have no faith in us and believe they can minimize our voices by keeping us up in arms — often referred to as a "race to the bottom of the brainstem" because we become polarized, defensive, and lose trust in one another.

Foremost, trust is how we begin building a foundation. Next, we gather around tables, attend town hall meetings, and communicate with elected officials. To problem solve, all ideas must be welcomed without judgment. And finally, we shape our solutions not based on the next season or the next four years, but rather a distant horizon — a goal as seemingly unfathomable as 2050 and the 50-Year Farm Bill.

Now you are invited to become part of the team. Subscribe, Like, spread the word any way you can. From the bottom of my heart — thank you.

Levi Lyle
Organic farmer of row crops and U-pick fruits
Keota, Iowa

Chapter 1: Caretaking

And on the 8th day, God looked down on his planned paradise and said, "I need a caretaker." So God made a farmer.
　　　　　　Paul Harvey, So God Made A Farmer (1978)

Every farmer shares some common appreciation for their role in something greater than him/herself. A farmer understands this in the blessing of rain that comes when most needed; a farmer feels the work of forces greater than himself in the emergence of sprouts stretching across an entire field; a farmer sees the greater power of nature's cycles in the changes to land and climate over the span of decades and generations.

But we, as farmers, have been deficient in our understanding of symbiotic relationships. While we cognitively grasp the art of forming parts into wholes, our efforts to preserve are ineffective in maintaining the integrity of the whole. Without integration of these historically ignored arts, our efforts of conservation will be in vain.

A Systems Approach

In 1808, the Industrial Revolution was just gaining its legs when a young scientist, Thomas Young, publicly posed a question during a lecture he was presenting on the diameter of branched blood vessels in the human body. He concluded with his findings that a ratio is consistently useful in predicting arterial wall diameter in relation to blood flow capacity.

One hundred and eighteen years later, a man by the name of Cecil D. Murray developed a formal principle for describing optimal dimensions for such systems, thereby demonstrating a uniformity in both living and non-living systems which had first been described by Young in his famous lecture. This principle became known as "Murray's Law."

In nature, natural order shows us again and again its predisposition toward interconnected and interdependent relationships. Systems of agriculture, if they are to meet the demands of our future, must, unwaveringly, be built upon principles of nature.

Two centuries after Young's first observations, the designers of modern systems are reluctant to accept the idea that, in nature, a whole is made up of disparate parts that, when addressed, individually lose the functional synergy of the whole.

Albert Howard, Aldo Leopold, and J. Russell Smith were prolific in disseminating the destructive impacts of neglecting nature's ecological systems in pursuit of production for agricultural means. As the pace of industrial farming quickened in the mid-twentieth century, their published works were widely available but largely ignored. The lure of a farming model based on exploitation of resources was contrary to the systems thinking described in Murray's Law (see "A Systems Approach").

Husbanding the fertility of land is synonymous to "caring" for it. As care is central to what makes a human, it is wise to know and understand that care for an ecosystem, which every acre of farmland contains within, must be informed by past care. In his book, *Our Only World*, Wendell Berry elegantly describes how, together, the past and present make up a heritage of skill with a future potential for adequate care. He calls this potential "caretaking."

Where a culture of caring for the land (husbandry) and its resources once resided, corporations now occupy. This occupation of the middle ground between economy and ecology is violent because it does not account for the environmental and human costs of production.

Large agricultural businesses supply "industrial inputs" and purchase a short list of commodity products. Within the state where I reside, Iowa, it's corn, soybeans, and pork. In this environment, multi-national agriculture corporations prosper unadulterated. Meanwhile, farmers, bearing the risk and labor, are the most exploited, least protected, and lowest paid.

It is essential that we challenge ourselves to make such intangible calculations. For it is the same intangible calculation required of "caretaking." And because they are intangible and do not meet the criteria of accounting ledgers, industrial agriculture cannot begin to address these questions, for efficiency, above all else, is king.

Among compassionate farmers who understand what is at stake, a movement for balance between economy and ecology has begun. On my farm, the twenty-five years of no-till, most of which my father was responsible for, was segue for a transition to the organic and regenerative practices that exemplify my commitment to caretaking.

When the only people who know the history, the heritage, and the uniqueness of the land are gone — who remains as caretakers?

My own contemplation of this question is fed by thoughtful advocates for systems thinking like Wendell Berry and Wes Jackson, whose ideas, no doubt, are sprinkled within my own writing. I have chosen the words of Paul Harvey to guide the telling of values in common in my own words. For this task, I begin as Harvey did, acknowledging a biblical first day, setting a foundation on which all else is built.

Chapter 2: Commitment

God said, "I need somebody willing to get up before dawn, milk cows, work all day in the fields, milk cows again, eat supper and then go to town and stay past midnight at a meeting of the school board." So God made a farmer.

To fulfill what our modern system of education presents as a goal implies that farmers' children must leave their roots in order to find prosperity.

Can rural life not support the brightest minds with the best ideas?

Can farming not challenge the imagination of our most skilled and creative people?

Are the youth who we devote our greatest hope to not suited to rural life?

These are rhetorical questions we know the answers to. Yet, we must acknowledge Albert Einstein's warning:.

"Insanity is doing the same thing over and over again and expecting different results."

—Albert Einstein

If one keeps doing the same things, making the same mistakes time and time again but expecting different results, it's time to change the way of thinking.

> - Just 16% of farmers are age 35 or under. These future leaders represent 240,141 farms.
> - Just 105,453 farms produced 75% of all sales in 2017, down from 119,908 in 2012.
> - The 1.56 million operations making under $50,000 represent just 2.9% of all sales.
>
> National Agricultural Statistics Service, 2017, USDA.

Young farmers see nothing to commit to in farming today, because we're stuck in the past. It's clear — our patterns of the past are not suited for the future. To continue to exalt a reverence for the industrial system is nothing short of insanity.

Now, as new technologies surrounding markets in climate change mitigation are emerging we have an opportunity to set things right. The monitoring, reporting, and verification (MRV) costs and standardizations of carbon estimations, for example, are synonymous with our obsession with making a new paradigm fit the old. We, as human beings, have a notorious tendency to dichotomize even when the situation doesn't fit. This is what we are doing in the industry of ecological services. As a result, we are not asking the most important question that needs to be answered.

How does MRV become a by-product of a functional system, rather than the basis of the functional system?

This invaluable question was first posed to me in a conversation with Christophe Jospe, one of the founders of Nori Carbon. Nori, created as a climate solutions company, is asking the right questions and Christophe is excellent at unpacking these questions anthropologically. Speaking with Christophe on the topic of MRV and what will be required to catalyze lasting change, I discovered he had been contemplating the same will-of-the-good approach I was writing a book about. He conceptualizes the dilemma in simplified terms of "do" versus "sell."

Shifting our thinking will require difficult personal work. As these important steps begin to unveil progress in how humans solve problems, an important outcome will be how we shift our individual consciousnesses to start confronting challenges beginning with "do" rather than an economic priority that begins with "sell" (www.cjospe.medium.com).

At the beginning of this chapter on "commitment," I posed three rhetorical questions about the potential of rural life to foster creative passion and connection. Without a doubt, the solutions, which have thus far proven elusive, will be solved by approaching with a "do" rather than "sell" approach in mind.

Einstein was known for his daydreaming, staring off into oblivion in deep wonder. Just as he may have, imagine you are free of the conditioning that natural selection once favored to win us our place as primates on our planet. Experiment placing yourself in a time about seventy million years ago, while the physiological mechanisms concerning fear, prioritized safety, food, and shelter, were in place but the emotional and social *hardwiring*, unique to primates, was not yet evolved.

This takes practice, but it's this sort of exercise that leads to experiments in art, science, and the sculpting of civilization. This is work we must do if we are to reshape our world—whether renewing relationships of balance with our natural environment or rekindling relationships within our human community, or re-shaping how we look at "do" versus "sell."

> **From the Heart of the Field**
>
> I live in Washington County, Iowa, and farm corn and soybeans, as well as niche fruit crops like honeyberries, tart cherries, and aronia berries. Along with my wife and children, I sell our products directly to market and manage our farm as a U-pick. Our row crops consist of 600 acres of corn and soybeans. Sixty acres of the 600 are devoted to organic certified corn and beans and the berry crops.
>
> Like many farm kids, after high school I left without a plan to return. More than ten years later, after college and graduate school at The University of Northern Iowa (UNI), and having worked as a high school biology teacher, social worker, and college coach, the arrival of children gave my wife and me a new perspective on life. Family would become our guiding light, both the candle illuminating the way and the guidepost to measure all of our activities.
>
> Thus, when we were offered the opportunity to move back to the community where we both had been raised, we knew doing so was the right decision. Both

of our families still resided on farms there. I knew I wanted to farm. And we were fortunate to have support and encouragement from my father, who still is actively involved in the farm's day-to-day operation. Without these, I would have faced barriers that discourage many young farmers from entering agriculture – high costs and limited access to farmland, large start-up investments, coping with lack of experience and market volatility – and I would have had difficulty getting started. Even with these aids, for a while I maintained an off-the-farm job while inspiration and effort paved the way toward full-time farming and organic agriculture.

From the start, I knew I needed to align my farming practices with what I felt was right. My life was showing me that how we farm, the prevalence of cancer, and the state of our environment are threads of a single story about our rural communities. Previously, as a running back on the UNI football team, I had experienced the power of food as medicine. My journey to achieve optimal physical performance, coupled with childhood memories of my father's diagnosis of cancer which he had successfully overcome, were at work within me.

I also remembered that when I was a child, in the 1980s, DDT had dramatically reduced bald eagle populations and the species was on the brink of extinction. In the years prior to moving back to the farm in 2010, I had only rarely seen bald eagles. After returning, I found populations had recovered, and eagles could be seen daily around the farm, sometimes even nesting high in old oak trees.

These realizations all supported my desire to farm organically, that is to grow crops without synthetic pesticides or fertilizers in accordance with the National Organic Program standards. And I also wanted to maintain an intimate connection to the land like my father and grandfathers had done. For me, this has meant remaining small scale and using farming practices that reflect nature's complex interconnections.

One extremely beneficial way I have done so is by combining the practices of no-till and planting cover crops with use of a device called a roller-crimper which allows a farmer to reduce or eliminate herbicide use while improving soil health. No-till is the agricultural practice of planting crops without disturbing the soil with tillage equipment. Cover crops, which are grown from fall until spring while the land would otherwise sit fallow, protect the soil from erosion and nutrient loss that would pollute water resources. Cover crops are often used as part of a no-till practice.

The roller-crimper is an implement attached to my tractor that lays the rye down, creating a weed suppressing mat. Five years ago, I began using the conservation no-till practice of roller-crimping rye on organic soybeans. I plant a rye crop in October, which grows through the winter. When the rye cover crop reaches maturity in early June, it is pushed down and "crimped" by the roller-crimper, effectively killing the cover crop without severing it from contact with the ground. Once the rye has been rolled and crimped, soybeans are planted directly into the rye. I accomplish all this by installing both a front-mounted roller-crimper and rear-mounted planter on the tractor, thus allowing me to do the whole operation in a single pass.

The one-pass approach has been crucial to improving my farming, my soils, and my profitability in many ways. It cuts down on my labor, reduces the use of fuel, and greatly reduces the soil compaction caused by tractors making many passes over the same ground as they plant and later spray the crops. What's more, while at first I limited use of the roller-crimper to my organic acres, I have since found I can profit by using the practice on my more extensive conventional acres. Thus, I have eliminated herbicide use across much of my entire soybean acreage.

Furthermore, by allowing the cover crop to remain alive in the soil as long as possible, the row crops reap multiple benefits. In addition to the cover-crop mulch suppressing weeds, I am putting armor on the topsoil and simultaneously creating the conditions to feed more soil microbes. By using no-till, cover cropping, and roller-crimping, I am protecting the soil from sunlight (which causes evaporation of water and gassing-off of carbon) and boosting carbon sequestration in the prairie-generated soils. I like to think of my actions as something like what the bison once may have done, their hooves knocking down the plants they did not eat and creating a soil-covering mat not unlike what's produced by my roller-crimper. (For this reason, I sometimes refer to the method of using a roller-crimper as the Bison System.) The boosting of carbon sequestration provides a valuable service to society by helping to mitigate climate change.

Questions of yields and profitability weigh heavily on any farmer. I have been incredibly happy with the amount of money I am saving by roller-crimping instead of using herbicide passes. Using these regenerative methods is improving my profits while also building soils and helping me address climate change.

For me, farming is also about safeguarding my family's health. I used to worry when I came home that my family would be exposed to insecticide and herbicide residues on my clothing. Now that worry is gone. Knowing that my children, who range in age from 5 to 13, can safely participate in farm activities is greatly rewarding. Also, I have begun to see the return of butterflies and bees in my fields.

Each season of the year has work my children can assist with. This is primarily mowing, maintaining, and harvesting the bushes where berry crops grow. Harvests are staggered by design, which means there is something new to pick and enjoy each month of the summer: honeyberries ripen in early June; tart cherries ripen in early July; Aronia berries ripen in late August.

(Reprinted with permission from Cornelia Mutel).

While many farmers profitably make the transition to organic production, I have seen that profitability alone is not enough to sustain a farmer's motivations. To endure the many challenges, I fall back on my commitment to a community that can support more small producers, which in turn support more local businesses to service those producers. This could mean the difference between keeping the local school open or seeing it close. It means giving the next generation an opportunity to farm. I hope to be part of a shift from an extractive agricultural paradigm to one of regenerative economics that values the most important system of all— that of our human communities. I endeavor to create value in principles that will remain staples of sustainable rural life: husbandry of the land and regenerative stewardship. It is these reasons, not just financial profits, that drive me to succeed.

My wife and I worry about climate change and the future opportunities for our son and daughters to farm. When speaking to farmer groups about solving the global greenhouse gas dilemma, a recurring theme of concern expressed by farmers is making their bottom-line and staying in business. For this reason, I believe the place to begin is by innovating Midwest farm policy to empower farmers to lead.

Harvey's second stanza visits the commitment of farmers who possess an ethic for hard work in their DNA and are proud of it. The steadfast commitment and pride in the farmers of our nation gives me confidence in our ability to successfully shift our current paradigm of exploitation to a system with greater lasting potential for future generations. I believe that improving the planet should and can be the number one focus of farmers everywhere. This means a system that better supports soil health, but also better enables our human communities to thrive.

Chapter 3: Neighborliness

"I need somebody with arms strong enough to rustle a calf and yet gentle enough to deliver his own grandchild. Somebody to call hogs, tame cantankerous machinery, come home hungry, have to wait lunch until his wife's done feeding visiting ladies and tell the ladies to be sure and come back real soon — and mean it." So God made a farmer.

Purchasing farm inputs as locally as is reasonable is a good way to provide neighborliness. Though local products are often at a premium in cost, the compounding impact of a single dollar circulating through the buying and selling of the local economy is quintessential to a robust community.

A good example on my farm is the purchase of seed corn, hybridized regionally. The geneticist and plant breeder who owns and operates the small business I buy my seed corn from left his position at one of the largest corn breeding and multinational chemical companies in the world. While there, he developed some of their top hybrids before one day deciding he could no longer knowingly submit to a philosophy of one size fits all corn breeding.

Now, he independently develops hybrids using localized

epigenetics he has spent his professional life developing for the microclimates of the central-southeast Iowa prairie. While stories of corn breeding for very regionalized areas are currently rare, a movement will form as farmers shift to a neighborly mindset, supporting local first whenever possible.

A second example is working with neighbors to fulfill seeding of cover crops and application of manure. Still, I find I have fewer and fewer neighbors, but year in and year out the land seems to always get farmed. There are those who attend school board meetings bent on pointing fingers and blaming rather than trying to understand the reasons why our schools risk closing or consolidating. Do they not notice their neighbors are fewer?

Answer: Public funding of education is delegated based on population; population is based on jobs; we continue to eliminate jobs within our community in the name of "efficiency" in agriculture. Better solutions require a shift in our thinking.

I believe a community could correct this situation by negotiating with farmers to sell acreages large enough to accommodate rural business enterprises to young families. Such purchases may even be subsidized by the local community chamber of commerce or state and local taxation. In one such scenario, if a family fulfills a commitment to a decade living on the tract and all the while conducting a rural business enterprise associated with the ten acres for example, a mortgage would be forgiven.

Once I have neighbors, it's up to me to endow neighborliness. The science of happiness shows niceness is good for health — those who give the most away reap the most benefit in both emotional and physical health. When seeking to uplift others, we are uplifted in the process. Neighborliness may further be conducive to self-interest if and when one day he/she stands in judgment before The Beholder.

> **From the Heart of the Field**
>
> *Excerpt taken from Ice Sage: Living and Loving the Land Prose (Forthcoming)* Journal of a twelve-year-old Levi Lyle
>
> For the greater part of a century, the massive barn located on our farm was used to store ear corn piled high into the rafters of the second story. My dad tells me stories from the time when he was my age. His father, Grandpa Lyle, shelled ears of corn in the dead of winter using a cabless tractor to operate the thresher. He says they worked from morning until night smothered in the dust from the machine and always worked in the cold.
>
> Friends and neighbors would gather and share in the work. It was an economic advantage to help out your neighbor because there was only one thresher which went from farm to farm, all hands-on deck meant it would arrive at your farm sooner.
>
> At mealtime, the men all ate together. Such gatherings were a fellowship in the reliance of neighbors on one another. It always took place over Thanksgiving and was "cold as hell."
>
> Grandpa sometimes talks about the days when horses were used to drive the elevator and corn thresher. As a boy, he was too young to feed the ears into the machine,

> so he was assigned the task of "driving the horsepower by keeping five teams circling 'round and 'round all the livelong day," he says. These memories give perspective to how much easier I have it than he did, but I do not tell them how I secretly understand that. I am actually grateful for living in this time.

Naturally, it's the painful and dreaded memories of working on the farm as a kid that in hindsight turn out to be among the most cherished. It bothers my wife and I that we may be raising our children in a way that is too permissive of the immediate gratification we see in our culture. In stanza three of Harvey's poem, I can identify hard work as the anecdote for complacency and immediate gratification. But maybe the treasure Harvey touches upon is that hard work, when accompanied with reliance on neighbors and people whom you care for, isn't so hard and can even be enjoyed.

Though the times have changed and my children won't know the kind of relentless duty required of the farm I knew as a boy, maybe I will do them the best honor by teaching them about the value of neighbors and reliance on community.

Chapter 4: Resourcefulness

God said, "I need somebody willing to sit up all night with a newborn colt. And watch it die. Then dry his eyes and say, 'Maybe next year.' I need somebody who can shape an ax handle from a persimmon sprout, shoe a horse with a hunk of car tire, who can make harness out of haywire, feed sacks and shoe scraps. And who, planting time and harvest season, will finish his forty-hour week by Tuesday noon, then, pain'n from 'tractor back,' put in another seventy-two hours." So God made a farmer.

Machines make ever more swift passage across the land as efficiency equates to quickness. First comes size and speed, later comes straightening of contours and natural obstructions. At first, it's trees and ponds pushed aside and filled in; later it's the dilapidated and abandoned homesteads. In such a way, the fate of local ecology and local economy are inseparable.

Wes Jackson, founder of the non-profit The Land Institute, developed the concept of an "eyes-to-acres ratio." This can be defined as eyes on the land to watch for signs of harm and to have a constant presence. Taken a step further, it can mean understanding the history of a place, to be aware of both the natural and human history. There is no way to compute the necessary ratio of eye-to-acres for a given place because of the many natural and human variables.

Diversity

On my farm, balancing risk through diversification helps alleviate financial risk. I grow and market perennial fruits such as honeyberries (June harvest), tart cherries (July harvest), and aronia berries (August harvest). These seasonal opportunities offer local products to the community and their staggered production means there is always something healthy to offer the market. Moreover, the ultimate benefit is the opportunity to engage my children in the rewards of hard work, together.

From the Heart of the Field

Case Study: "Aronia Berries—Good for Health, the Land and Smaller Farms" By Dan Ehl, *The Kalona News*, March 27, 2014

Levi Lyle was taking a walk with his 1-year-old daughter Olivia when he noticed an unfamiliar berry bush in an Indianola neighbor's yard. That was in 2008. He had no idea that the berry would bring him home earlier than expected to the family farm north of Keota. A hint was his daughter's first response to the purple aronia berries.

"Olivia, who resided in my backpack, reached for a handful of her own," says Levi on his website for Levi's Indigenous Fruit Enterprises. "At first, I thought she would cower at the tart flavor of the aronia berry. To the contrary, she couldn't get enough. Soon her entire mouth and fingers were stained with aronia's rich purple juice."

Levi, a graduate of the University of Northern Iowa with a master's degree in student administration, was at Simpson College that year where he prepared low-income students for college in a program called Upward Bound. He was also a football coach at Simpson.

Later in 2008, Levi with wife Jill and parents Trent and Joy, planted one acre of aronia bushes on the Keota farm that goes back six generations.

Last year the Lyles harvested 1,000 pounds of the berries. This year, with the 1,000 bushes maturing, Levi said he hopes to harvest twice or three times that amount.

What's so special about the aronia berry? Native and therefore well adapted to Iowa's soils, the purple fruit is known to be rich in antioxidants including anthocyanins. Studies have shown that these pigments have properties associated with reduced systemic inflammation – a key factor in the development of chronic diseases. Levi says the aronia berry has one of the highest amounts of anthocyanins in the fruit world. "Eating aronia berries has reduced my inflammation from playing college football."

"Basic research on aronia consumption identifies the potential for reducing risk of disease," states Wikipedia. Among the models under evaluation include reduction of blood cholesterol, colorectal cancer, cardiovascular disease, chronic inflammation, gastric mucosal disorders (peptic ulcer), eye inflammation (uveitis) and liver failure.

The bushes on the Lyle family will mature at 6 to 8 feet in height and 5 to seven feet in width. The bushes need no pesticides or tilling of the soil, which reduces soil erosion. Maintenance is mostly mowing and pruning. He has been told the best three ways to prevent rodent and skunk predation are mowing, mowing and mowing. Over the winter and early spring there have been 10 eagles perching in a maple tree near the bushes. He watched one eagle snatch a rabbit.

"Seeing an eagle watch over our crop is kind of surreal," he said.

Levi's organic certified berries are sold fresh at area farmers markets, at Hy-Vee stores and at JW's Foods in Kalona when in season. The berries are also sold at the New Pioneer Coop stores in Iowa City and Coralville, Everybody's Whole Foods in Fairfield and the Golden Dome Market in Fairfield.

Though aronia berries look similar to blueberries, the fruit has a tart taste of its own, Levi said. They are often used in salads and smoothies, or as Levi's father does, on cereal.

Picking the berries is labor intensive – taking about 2 hours to fill a 5-gallon bucket that holds approximately 25 pounds. All told, said Levi, it took about 40 hours last year to complete the harvest. With some of their neighbors also planting aronia bushes, there are plans to go in together to buy a mechanical harvester that is similar to ones used for blueberries.

Still, said Levi, picking by hand has its advantages. Such harvesting allows a continued picking through the several-week period as the individual berries ripen.

Daughters Olivia and Elyse have helped in the harvesting, Levi observed, but so far they usually eat most of what they pick. "They get pretty purple." Son Emerson is still too young to follow his sisters.

"I thought it was kind of crazy," laughs Trent about first being told of his son's idea for planting and marketing the berry, but added that with agricultural operations continuing to grow larger, it will take something different to survive on smaller farms. Only corn and soybeans were grown on the Lyle farm, Trent having decided not to expand into hog confinement a number of years ago.

"Raising my family on a smaller farm, just as my father and grandfather did, is the most fulfilling life," Levi says. "The only option is to diversify," he concluded.

The mission statement of his effort says much:

Levi's Indigenous Fruit Enterprises recognizes the farmer as the keeper of balance between man and nature. Farmers respect and uphold the natural capacity of the landscape. The role of our farm is to deliver wholesome, fully ripe, fruit to the consumer with optimal nutritive value. Three practices epitomize and sustain LIFE.

- Organic growing
- Perennial, native Iowa fruits
- Local distribution of products

There is a story in my family that goes back several generations. It was told not by my great grandfather, but by his neighbor who later asked my grandparents, who in 1965 were just scraping by and had a family of seven young children, to cropshare his farm. It was an opportunity that made the difference between success and failure at the time to my grandparents:

"In 1912, father wanted me to take over management of the place. One of the first questions I asked was, "How much can I reasonably expect to make out of the farm?"

"A living," he replied.

"How much is that?" I wanted definitive figures.

"Well, you know how we live as well as I do."

In stanza four, Harvey gives an account of the resourcefulness of a farmer. Resourcefulness develops out of a necessity to be efficient, to solve problems working with what you have on hand. In farm management, the ultimate resourcefulness is the ability to manage risk. Risk management is a primary concern of the farmer highlighted in the excerpt. In a sense, growing organic perennial fruit crops like aronia berries, tart cherries, and honeyberries is resourceful just as "shaping an ax handle from a persimmon sprout, shoe a horse with a hunk of car tire, or making harness out of haywire, feed sacks and shoe scraps…." It is no coincidence these things are good for the soil and healthy for my family and community, while at the same time improving my farm by implementing diversity. In this aspect, Harvey's words ring as clear today as when he wrote them.

> Through the USDA, Conservation Innovation Grants, Value Added Producer Grants, Specialty Crop Block Grants, and other programs incentivize efforts in resourcefulness among farmers. Also, organizations such as Practical Farmers of Iowa and Iowa Soybean Association are making headway supporting the diversification of farm enterprises. Through these leading organizations, learn about the Cover Crop Business Accelerator Program to get assistance developing business plans.

Chapter 5: Balance

God had to have somebody willing to ride the ruts at double speed to get the hay in ahead of the rain clouds and yet stop in mid-field and race to help when he sees the first smoke from a neighbor's place. So God made a farmer.

Successful eyes-to-acres can delegate a balance in the scale of an operation. At the right scale, a farm is able to support the local economy and integrate with the local human community. While an eyes-to-acres ratio implies a limit to farm size, that limit implies a balance in the livestock to crop ratio which tends toward interdependence and symbiosis. My highly diversified farm is evidence that an appropriate eyes-to-acres ratio provides the necessary husbandry of local land. Also, an appropriate eyes-to-acres ratio on my farm has allowed greater flexibility and adaptation when necessary while growing my contact and connection with the land.

One such eyes-to-acres approach is coalescing the planting of my soybean crop with cover crop rolling in a single pass. I conduct this with a front mounted roller crimper— uniting the "Bison System" with one-pass farming.

> **What is cover crop rolling?**
> Cover crop rolling is an advanced no-till technique. Typically, it involves flattening a high-biomass cover crop to produce a thick, uniform mat of mulch. A cash crop is then planted into the mulch. The rolling process itself will kill the cover crop while leaving the biomass and root structures intact. This means burndown herbicides can be reduced or eliminated.
>
> Cover crop rolling has been used for decades on millions of cropland acres in South America. With the adoption of a culture around cover cropping, cover crop rolling is becoming more widespread in the U.S. (USDA Natural Resource Conservation Service)

In the years prior to adopting this approach, the fields required a pre-emergent herbicide pass prior to going to the field with the planter. This meant each time I left the safety of the cab I was being exposed to harmful herbicides. These herbicides, for example Valor™ and Fierce™ manufactured by Sumitoma Chemical Company and Authority™ and Warrant™ manufactured by Bayer BASF, to name a few, last all season long, killing weeds into late summer. I wondered, "How long do the residues remain on my boots and clothes when I go home to my family?" As a result, I sought to remain in the tractor as much as possible. This premise of course goes counter to the eyes-to-acres philosophy.

Sustainability

Now I am profiting by refraining from use of pre-emergent herbicides in fields where I use a one-pass farming approach. As a result, unlike other soybean fields in my area, I do not have weed problems. Without the herbicide resistant weeds, I've eliminated the use of genetically modified organism (GMO) seeds too, which were more expensive anyway. These GMO seeds are branded as "double and triple stacked genetic modifications," and "XtendFlex" brand, which has Liberty, Roundup, and Dicamba (all post emergent herbicides) resistant gene modifications.

Fuel savings are a result of eliminating a herbicide pass, often twice when conditions are more dry like in 2020, and planting and rolling cover crop in one pass. This is not to mention the greenhouse gas (GHG) reduction, using less fuel by roller crimping rye in a one pass equipment configuration. Then, in addition to using less or sometimes no herbicides, I have found that planting later (during the first ten days of June) consistently results in immediate emergence because soil temperatures are more favorable. Delayed planting eliminates the need for neonicotinoid pesticidal seed coatings, intended to protect against nematodes. This allows for the purchase of cheaper, non-coated soybean seeds that are non-GMO, a requirement of organic production. As neonicotinoid pesticidal seed coatings are notoriously associated with the decline of the honeybee and dangerous to handle with bare hands, it's an easy choice.

The ability to compete with conventional systems is tied up with the question of yields and profitability, a consideration that weighs heavily on any farmer. However, using these regenerative methods is improving our profits. Traditionally, farmers in this region make two herbicide passes in their fields. In recent years, some have resorted to three, sometimes four trips, and they still have weeds due to herbicide resistance.

It's clear: one pass farming leads to fewer herbicides. This allows later planting and elimination of pesticides. These together lead to fuel savings and less expensive seed inputs. All these lead to an economic advantage.

To me, the intangible benefit of being able to touch the seeds I am planting is part of the eyes-to-acres philosophy as well. I used to worry when I came home that my family would be exposed to pesticide and herbicide residues on my clothing. Now that worry is gone. Also, I have begun to see the return of butterflies and bees in my fields. Further, feeling like my children, who range in age from 5-13, can safely participate in the farm is greatly rewarding.

Because there is no way to compute an eye-to-acres ratio, one can not offer a recommendation of what would constitute an appropriate ratio on your farm. There are geographic and ecological variables, differences in seasons and climate from place to place, as well as human variables that make it impossible to predict a one size fits all ratio. Even distinctions between neighbors' fields are significant. Nonetheless, the absoluteness of a need for eye-to-acres possesses a force not unlike Murray's Law.

From the Heart of the Field

Excerpt taken from *Ice Sage: Living and Loving the Land Prose (Forthcoming)*

A sip of coffee. Another sip. And another. Another cup. Trent wanted life to go back to the way things had been just a few hours ago before he learned that he was going to die from cancer. Now, sitting at his mom's kitchen table, he knew there was no going back. After enough delay, his mother asked what it was that he was not telling her. He explained to his mom that the doctors told him he might die.

A thousand times he had sat at that table, but never before had he so appreciated the value of small talk. Seemingly irrelevant: the weather, the crops, the pigs and sheep, life as usual was long gone. He spoke. "The doctors say there is an experimental treatment called chemotherapy. They use a fungus from the soil and plant alkaloids from coneflowers. They will inject my veins with the hormones. They will take out the disease. I will lose my hair."

Trent did not want to go home to Joy. How do you tell your wife that you are going to die? It pained him to imagine his three children growing up without a dad.

Anne was in first grade, Emily in kindergarten, and Levi still a toddler. He thought, if I die my boy will not be old enough to remember who I am. I don't want my children to grow up without a dad. Before his testicle was finally removed, it had swollen to the size of a giant sweet potato.

The surgical incision, located near his hip, was five inches long. He lost a testicle but still had the other. At the local places farmers regularly commence, feed store, livestock auctions, and taverns, he would joke about it with a motive to make sure people knew: one healthy nut intact!

He lost his hair. The chemotherapy, another poison with a different purpose, had the task of destroying the rogue cells within his body. Doctors said his healthy mitochondria should withstand the treatments. In theory, but who really knew. The cancer had advanced to his lungs, the illness had advanced to stage four. Usually at stage four they send you home and tell you to enjoy each day of your life to the fullest because the damage to your body is irreconcilable.

※ ※ ※

During the spring of 1984, Joy learned to cultivate six inch high corn. She had just been accepted into the University of Iowa. She and Trent decided she may need to prepare for a life as the sole provider for her family and that is the reason she enrolled. Joy did what she could to keep the farm going while Trent was in the hospital receiving treatment. Anne, Emily, and Levi were eight, six, and five.

Why weave personal stories of crisis into Harvey's portrayal of "balance?" How does hardship relate to eyes-to-acres or sustainability?

What Harvey portrays as balance is actually inseparable from the threshold of resilience on a farm. Without balance, which is evidenced by right eyes-to-acres ratio, the flexibility and adaptability of a farm becomes vulnerable. However, as my family can attest, where there is balance seemingly impossible barriers can be overcome.

Chapter 6: Stewardship

God said, "I need somebody strong enough to clear trees and heave bails, yet gentle enough to tame lambs and wean pigs and tend the pink-combed pullets, who will stop his mower for an hour to splint the broken leg of a meadow lark. It had to be somebody who'd plow deep and straight and not cut corners. Somebody to seed, weed, feed, breed and rake and disc and plow and plant and tie the fleece and strain the milk and replenish the self-feeder and finish a hard week's work with a five-mile drive to church.

There is a significant and obtuse change in ecology of the land near which I have lived most of my life. The changes that are clearly apparent to me are perfectly invisible to nearly everybody else.

The streams where I chased mudpuppies, a threatened species of salamander, as a boy once carried water all year around. Mudpuppies are dark red with black spots, have four digits on their arms and legs, and a paddle-like tail. Even in winter, the streams carried dangerous current beneath their frozen surface which I can attest to. Once I fell through the ice and was nearly swept beneath.

To people who have no intimacy with the local land, they

look and see beauty—the waving knee-high corn and the lush fields appear impeccably clean from the roadside. These outsiders have no perspective, no memory, which causes them to see things as normal. But there is nothing normal about it. Due to the many miles of tile and terracing that remove water quickly and efficiently from the agriculture landscape, the streams are dried up all but a few weeks out of the year. Today, the only aquatic life is toads and dragonflies that make an appearance for a brief time each spring.

Un-sustainability

Disregard for the impact our way of life has on the natural world means we rarely speak of "human costs," "collateral damages," or "ecological costs." When we finally get around to using verbiage such as "unsustainable," too often what we mean is unsustainable in maintaining that luxurious "way of life," rather than the unsustainable effect humans have on natural ecological systems. This is less than remorseful. Do we still not acknowledge our thoughtlessness and carelessness even in retrospect?

Regenerative

Practices such as cover crop rolling and weed zapping, a practice which uses high voltage electricity powered by a tractor power take-off, can be classified as regenerative AND sustainable. However, I distinguish between the two by speaking of sustainability from a profitability vantage point in chapter five. For example, Syngenta, one of the largest agricultural suppliers in the world, exploits nature in its fundamental premise by producing herbicides, fungicides, and insecticides. Still, the corporation uses "sustainability" language in its marketing, diversifying into biofuels in recent years. It would be a mistake to misconstrue this as a path toward "regenerative" or "ecological balance."

Hence, sustainability has become a marketing word which too often is used as a smokescreen to refer only to sustainable profits for shareholders. Profits are important and must be sustainable, but that is not necessarily regenerative.

Economist John Fullerton, in his book *Regenerative Capitalism*, takes a look at regenerative through the lens of a former career as an investment banker for JP Morgan. Referring to the "Edge Effect Abundance," a phenomenon in which creativity, diversity, and life thrive on the edges of defined systems, he gives the example of the salty marsh tributaries where rivers and ocean meet. It is an environment where the bonds holding the dominant pattern of river versus ocean are the weakest. Crediting the work of Allan Savory and the Savory Institute he explains, "where proper regenerative stewardship is in place, the edges embody strong innovation and cross-fertilization" (Fullerton, 2015). This premise holds true whether the "edge" is the tributaries of the Mississippi or the boundary where my corn fields meet the stream.

"Regenerative economics" is a way of thinking about economic assets built on the principles of ecosystems and the human body. Its bottom line is very different from global capitalism's pursuit of short-term profit by acquiring and consuming. That way of thinking is "extractive," says Fullerton. And it's at the heart of the vast wealth divide and climate change crisis.

Regenerative economics instead sees economies as living systems that need to honor relationships to all other living systems. They need to be sustainable over long periods of time, rather than endlessly exploited. Another word for this is a "living economy."

From the Heart of the Field

Excerpt taken from *Ice Sage: Living and Loving the Land Prose (Forthcoming)*

Following one hell of a hailstorm, my father and I went to the fields. There we were met by the insurance adjuster.

Crop insurance works like this: if the bullet-sized holes in the leaves amount to yield-loss severity, the adjuster is the person who writes up the report for a claim to be paid. Upon arriving, the first thing I noticed about the guy is that he walked with a limp. It was a quarter-mile walk to get into the middle of the eighty acres, and the corn was knee-high.

He mentioned bein' a vet. I inquired if he had a service-related injury. It was a struggle to watch as he hobbled along, trying to lift his bad leg over the headland rows that ran perpendicular to us. After twenty-four straining grunts from him, we reached the long, straight rows that ran the length of the field. It was then that he began to talk. He was forthcoming with his story.

It was one that struck me as most incredible, and more importantly, ignited a shift in my thinking about the farm.

"As a State Trooper, I was struck by a car while writing a ticket during a routine stop. At the scene where I lay unconscious, a passer-by truck driver saw an opportunity to steal an issued 40mm. I was coming in and out of consciousness. I couldn't move or speak. I had my hand on the holster in a struggle with him. Another trucker, who saw what was unfolding from his rig, came onto the scene. He was 6'6" and 300 pounds. He knew some guys would try to get their hands on a cop-issued pistol to sell on the black market."

"Unlawful sons-a-bitches. They prize spitting on civility. The next and last thing I remember was this angel of a man lifting the no good S.O.B. to toss him skyward like a twig. It was poetry to see him rise like a bird, a dove or maybe a lark, up, up through the air on that arc. In my drifting consciousness, I swear I saw a rainbow like the tail of a comet as he disappeared over the top of the semi-trailer, clearing it by ten feet. Though my leg was shattered, I would be okay. This samaritan had saved my life. The best thing was that he came to see me in the hospital, and I was able to thank him."

It was a long walk through the field, and he continued. "That was just one life I went through; it seems like I've gotten off like a cat with nine. I was shot six times as a Seal before I was honorably discharged."

Surprised, I confirmed: "A seal?"

"Navy Seal. That's when I became a Trooper."

"How did you become a Seal?" I asked.

"I was in basic training when, after a three-day sleep deprivation test, my sergeant called me in and said I ought to apply to become a Seal. One year later, I was undercover ops doing drug cartel intel down in Columbia. During that stint, I was shot in my shoulder." He reached over and held his left shoulder. "Here, in my thigh," he placed his hand on his right hip. "I was hit in my groin, my neck, and the one in my belly just missed my spine. My job was to take down the bad guys or die trying. I shouldn't be here."

This seemed unbelievable to me, but there was no reason that this man would blow smoke up my ass. I wanted to be respectful and didn't probe any deeper. But I think there was some strong need compelling him to tell his story. To survive emotionally, I think he had to get his suffering out, and that's the reason he was such an open book. I think he sought to leave his torments out in the open fields. The powerful thing that came through in his voice was how he spoke so humbly. He did not say these things to impress.

He continued, "I was wired, got found out, and the shit went down. We (all Seals) carry tampons as part of the standard gear to plug bullet holes in our bodies; when you get hit, you quickly plug the wound. Tampons are amazing; they get you back into the fight."

I then realized maybe being an insurance adjuster was the perfect job for this guy. His soul seemed to have a need for wide-open space and the tranquility only nature can provide. He was speaking as to leave his story out there in the field. I wondered whether he'd be telling this stuff to the corn if no companions were beside him. In his line of work now, he walks a lot of fields by himself.

We were walking down near the creek where there were many birds, and we could here hear water draining from tile. This is also where gullies fester. My youth was spent tearing woven wire fence from the field borders to farm fence row to fence row. This results in surmounting rolls of wire that were placed into these gullies, a bone yard of sorts. Where gullies once ravaged, now these giant rolls absorb into the Earth among a tangle of sagebrush and birch. They plug wounds just the way tampons did for this Seal. I think of the fertility of the farm as Gaia, the ancestral Mother Earth; the importance of lunar cycles, a reset that is the emergence from winter and the entering of spring, and the steady growth of crops like the un-reprising care of a mother. But erosion is not menstruation.

How does stewardship move forward?

I find truth in Wendell Berry's conclusion in the purpose of industrial technology. The goal of industrialization has always been to cheapen work to increase the flow of wealth from the less wealthy to the more wealthy. We named, even disguised, the subsequent discombobulation of our rural communities favorably as labor-saving, efficient, progressive, fast, and convenient. We behaved as though all the gains of technological progress are net gains, says Berry in his collection of essays titled *Our Only World*. Generations of farmers before us weren't focused on whether there would be losers in the industrialization of our farms. Many farmers were, and still are, operating on a shoestring budget trying to make a living.

It is throwing spears to claim responsibility solely lies on the shoulders of the chemical industry, where farms spend $15 billion each year (USDA National Agricultural Statistics Service, 2019). It's more accurate to say the consciousness of a people under a veil of national righteousness and defense of freedom is now understood to be thoughtless and careless. To allude to our national interests is not making excuses for past actions. Understanding how our actions have gotten us to the depravity of our current circumstances will help us correct our mistakes and set the path right for future generations.

Regenerative Capitalism points out as fundamental that we must embrace this truth at every scale. You can not conceptualize stewardship top down, ignoring that regenerative has a human community component that synergizes with the whole system either. In the state of our current world, it would be a catastrophic mistake to think about stewardship in "the local" while forgetting about the macro scale of economy in John Fullerton's *Regenerative Capitalism*.

As I near a conclusion retrospectively looking at Harvey's living words, the final chapters on Balance, Stewardship, and Legacy are considerate of this holism.

Chapter 7: Legacy

Somebody who'd bale a family together with the soft strong bonds of sharing, who would laugh and then sigh, and then reply, with smiling eyes, when his son says he wants to spend his life doing what dad does. So God made a farmer.

Farmers assume the greatest risk while receiving the lowest income. Ever fewer farmers' children desire to farm.

> - The average age of all producers is 57.5, up 1.2 years from 2012.
> - The average age of producers who have served in the military is 67.9.
> - The average age of beginning farmers, those with fewer than 10 years of experience, is 46.3.
>
> USDA National Agricultural Statistics Service, 2017.

As of 2019, there were about 779 certified organic farms among Iowa's 86,000 total farms. Despite the many examples of success, there is much skepticism in the agricultural community about the feasibility of organic at the scale of chemical production alternatives (USDA National Agricultural Statistics Service, 2019). The merit of USDA-certified organic farms in moving toward a culture of regenerative practices need not polarize us. The larger movement farmers will trend toward is one of biological, ecological, and low-input methodology in its many forms.

A Movement Toward Balance

The need for farming to provide for future generations is inherent. A farmer may interpret this to mean instilling a connection to the land in his/her children or contributing to a food system that supports regenerative systems with a long range view. Whether looking at the matter from a micro or macro economic perspective, it makes sense to take a hard look at the undeniable potential of perennial plant production. Prairie roots add organic matter to the soil every year and the majority remain living all year around (Woida, 2021).

The foremost advocate for the development of perennial grains is The Land Institute. Deep-rooted, long-lived perennial crops, when grown on the 70% of crop land now growing annual monocultures, could reverse ecological damage to agricultural land, namely soil erosion, poisoning by pesticides, and biodiversity. The Land Institute promotes that conservation while providing adequate production is dependent on the continued progress of research into developing perennial grains (www.landinstitute.org).

The Land Institute proposal for a 50-Year Farm Bill is gaining momentum. The question, "Must conservation be at the expense of production?" has been asserted. The conclusion reached by The Land Institute is supported by thirty years of research and advocacy.

The Land Institute Proposal for A 50-Year Farm Bill.

A 50-Year Farm Bill would be a program using 5-year farm bills as milestones, systematically adding eight larger, more sustainable end goals to existing programs.

- Protect soil from erosion
- Cut fossil fuel dependence to zero
- Sequester carbon
- Reduce toxins in soil and water
- Manage nitrogen carefully
- Reduce dead zones
- Cut wasteful water use
- Preserve or rebuild farm communities

(www.landinstitute.org, 2009)

Honoring the History and Legacy of Land

There is a need for continual assessment on farms. This can be accomplished through on-farm practical research. Through efforts to contribute to a larger body of knowledge, I share my research in the public domain by conducting trials. When possible, I utilize partnerships with Iowa State University, The Native Fruit Association, Sustainable Agriculture Research and Education (SARE), and USDA programs such as Environmental Quality Incentives Program (EQIP). Also though, I contribute creatively to pass on an oral history of my farm. I aim to accomplish the need for land to have a legacy through the stories, songs, poems, and the like which I produce and publish. It is in the context of a holistic, or otherwise symbiotic, regenerative paradigm that still gives hope to Harvey's words.

Conclusion

Paul Harvey's description of rural life from 1978 seems, on first listen, like a missive from a lost past. Mechanization, industrialization, and the pursuit of efficiency above all have seemed to corrode the traditional values of the American farmer.

My goal in this writing is not to mourn the days past — but look forward to a bright future. The ideals that Harvey spoke of in 1978, as I hope I have shown, still exist on American farms today. All we need is a bit of creative problem-solving and a reverence for the land and our place in the natural order.

Industrial land use is not a war against the living world. Nature is not even a casualty to our violent and destructive ways. We are on the cusp of change which has always been our natural course.

Yes, we have been asleep. But now we are not. Paul Harvey's words are a cadence that provides the steadfast rhythm to renew rural America.

In my seemingly out of place anecdote about the 1980 Gold Medal U.S. Hockey Team and quotes from Vince Lombardi and Albert Einstein, I am making the case that complex problems require a shift in thinking to solve. We recognize obstacles in their archetypal form when considering the following multiple-choice question:

Who were the more formidable opponents of the 1980 U.S. Hockey team?

A. U.S.S.R.

B. The inner voice of doubt

This is not a trick question. As promised, the answer justifies my reason for drawing a parallel to *Miracle on Ice*. Think about that voice of doubt at times each of us has experienced. To overcome such self-destructive thinking, we must think like Vince Lombardi did. We, individually, must understand that our biggest adversary is closer to home than we are inclined to believe.

The inability to delay gratification and fulfillment of destructive self-prophecy was the epic opponent of the '80 Olympic Hockey Team— not the U.S.S.R.

No purpose + No will =

inability to delay gratification =

fulfillment of destructive self-prophecy =

subsequent failure of the goal

This, in fact, is the unexpected parallel between Olympic hockey and farming I mentioned earlier. If you lack a will to succeed and your purpose is unclear, you will circle the metaphorical Monopoly board happy tabulating your $200 each time around the game board, and nothing more.

The nemesis of solving the destruction-of-land-and-people dilemma is ourselves. The solution is within a spirit of renewal and our commitment to the principles we set forth together.

The voice of Paul Harvey is still in my head even after all these years. Many a summer I spent on the cabless International 1206 mowing, raking, and bailing hay listening to Paul Harvey's weekly commentary "The Rest of the Story," on the fender mounted AM radio. I believe those experiences, which seemed to instill the spirit of Paul Harvey's words in my fertile young mind, have reinforced something of the values he so cherished into my DNA, right alongside those instilled by my rural upbringing with a focus on family. Paul Harvey was there week after week, in and out of seasons, through the years of my youth.

In the ever expanding drive toward greater and greater efficiencies in agriculture, some believe the values Paul Harvey spoke of have been lost. For the reasons stated in this writing, I am hopeful the vision Paul Harvey had of the "American Farmer" is alive and well. It is the action of tomorrow's farmers which will indeed tell "the rest of the story."

Appendix A: Climate Leadership

Acknowledging "Exemplary 8"

For longer than I've been alive, the values and visionary people my ideas are built upon have been at work. Driven by a labor of love and a sense of responsibility and service, the effort put forth by these individuals has indeed been tireless and thankless. While it's impossible to name all the people and organizations that have made (and are making) a difference, I think of eight exemplary organizations I want to acknowledge because of their undisputed role, to facilitate change in agriculture. Together, referring to them in the name I've coined as *"Exemplary 8,"* they embody the values and consciousness of a new thinking. I name them along with their vision statements.

1. Understanding Agriculture, LLC

    Understanding Ag is a regenerative agricultural consulting company that provides the support and confidence to help our clients reduce input costs, generate actual profits, and ensure family farming futures. We accomplish this by educating and mentoring farmers, ranchers, landowners, businesses, and communities in the principles and practices needed to restore, repair, rebuild, and regenerate their farming and ranching ecosystems (www.understandingag.com).

2. The Land Institute

    The Land Institute is a non-profit organization based in Salina, Kansas, that was founded in 1976. The Land Institute's work, led by a team of plant breeders and ecologists in multiple partnerships worldwide, is focused on developing perennial grains, pulses and oilseed bearing plants to be grown in ecologically intensified, diverse crop mixtures known as perennial polycultures. The Institute's goal is to create an agricultural system that mimics natural systems in order to produce ample food and reduce or eliminate the negative impacts of industrial agriculture (www.landinstitute.org).

3. Practical Farmers of Iowa

    Practical Farmers of Iowa's mission is equipping farmers to build resilient farms and communities. Practical Farmers of Iowa is an inclusive organization representing a diversity of farmers. Farmers in our network raise corn and soybeans, hay, livestock large and small, horticultural crops from fruits and vegetables to cut flowers and herbs, and more. Our members have conventional and organic systems; employ diverse management practices; run operations of all sizes; and come from a range of backgrounds. These farmers come together, however, because they believe in nature as the model for agriculture and they are committed to moving their operations toward sustainability (www.practicalfarmers.org).

4. The Rodale Institute

    Rodale Institute is a 501(c)(3) nonprofit dedicated to growing the organic movement through rigorous research, farmer training, and consumer education. Widely recognized as the birthplace of the organic movement, Rodale Institute has been the global leader in regenerative organic agriculture for over 70 years (www.rodaleinstitute.org).

5. Carbon6CSA

    The mission of Carbon6CSA is to carry out GHG Mitigation through Community Sponsored Agriculture. You cannot "policy" a shift in consciousness. Understanding our relationship with Earth's Biosphere is a cultural shift within our communities. To us, "ecological services," such as cover crops and nutrient management, are characteristics of a functional system rather than stand-ins to create the appearance of functional natural cycles (www.carbon6csa.com). See "Appendix B" for more information on Carbon6CSA.

6. The Climate Reality Project

    Our mission is to catalyze a global solution to the climate crisis by making urgent action a necessity across every sector of society (www.climaterealityproject.org).

7. Real Organic

    Grassroots, farmer-led movement created to distinguish

soil-grown and pasture-raised products under USDA Organic. Our mission is to grow people's understanding of foundational organic values and practices; crops grown in soil and livestock raised on pasture are *fundamental* to organic (www.realorganicproject.org).

8. The Native Fruit Association
   The Native Fruit Association (NFA) was formed to promote and share knowledge about native fruits of the Midwest that have commercial possibilities (www.nativefruit.org).

Much could be said about the specific mission of each of these organizations. Each has distinguishable characteristics which are succinct to their cause. The overarching values of the "The Exemplary 8" results in a vision which epitomizes the future of our human and ecological communities.

While the private investment world is forging headlong into agricultural opportunities in climate change by investing billions, they ignore important fundamentals. Right scale; eyes-to-acres; neighbors; caretaking; and stories of the people, land's geography, and its change, are intangible. These elements impart an economic advantage to human communities which does not immediately show on ledgers of return-on-investment (ROI). In this book, these concepts have been highlighted in the promise of leaving the wilderness better than it was before.

Appendix B

Carbon6CSA's Six Principles of Agriculture to Accompany GHG Mitigation

Carbon6CSA has been developed using a CSA business model because of the unity of two aspects: "action" and return on investment (ROI). For the community of CSA subscribers, this has proven effective.

In farming, as in any business, just feeling good is not a long-term sustainable strategic plan. Carbon6CSA's Six Principles of Agriculture to Accompany GHG Mitigation coalesce to mimic natural systems and their forms. Carbon6CSA's six principles are based on the study of nature.

Neighborliness

Examples of neighborliness could be described by a farm as generally as purchasing farm inputs locally, partnering in share agreements with neighbors for equipment use, or mentoring a beginning farmer. Maybe your household pledges to purchase a percentage of groceries locally. Maybe you are a coach or a local youth group leader at your church. Any action which improves the relationship with neighbors and community and supports others locally would meet the characteristic of a good neighbor.

Diversity

There are many facets to diversity on the farm. Like the multiple ways to define sustainability, so too can diversity be represented in ways which are separate and distinct. First, there is the importance of diverse microbiology in the soil, then there is the diversity which comes with an intact dynamic ecological system, finally there is the diversity of farm enterprises.

To Carbon6CSA, the principle of diversity within the six key approaches to CSA Member farms is intended to mean diversity of farm enterprises. A diverse farm is actually multiple small businesses, season by season, with emphasis on specific crops and practices at different times of year. Integration of grazing livestock is one of many forms of diversification of farm enterprises. From an enterprise standpoint, diversity helps alleviate risk, but also can play an important role in the local civic community where a farmer markets products.

Sustainability

Simply defined, sustainability is the ability to exist indefinitely. For regenerative farmers, practices must be married to profitability. Awareness of the interaction between 1) farming practices intended to mitigate GHG, 2) crop production, and 3) bottom line economics inform a Carbon6CSA farmer of the sustainability of his/her farm operation. Among these three, the bottom line is not to be short changed, but instead is on par with other aspects.

Regenerative

Regenerative agriculture emphasizes rebuilding soil organic matter and restoring degraded soil biodiversity—resulting in both GHG mitigation and improving of natural nutrient cycle, water infiltration, and a soil's water holding capacity.

Fundamental principles of regenerative agriculture include minimal soil disturbance (primarily through the use of no-till, but not exclusively), maintaining living roots as armor in the soil year-round, diversification of crops and crop species, and integration of animals (traditionally grazing).

Caretaking

Care is central to what makes a human. On a spectrum ranging from analysis at one end to the love capable by the human heart on the other, caretaking solely lies on the side with love. Still, there must be skill, otherwise one will not know what he is looking at. What should ecology look like from one particular landscape to the next, for example?

Heritage, son and daughter journeymen and women in apprentice, is the most adequate preparation for gaining needed skills in caretaking. Furthermore, adequate caretaking is most strongly presented in a case for the right scale. What is necessary for properly nurturing a farm undoubtedly varies from one place to another because of the many environmental and human variables.

Honoring the History and Legacy of Land

To honor land, continual assessment is required of farms. This can be accomplished through on-farm practical research for example. Efforts to contribute learned knowledge to a larger body of farmers is an example of honoring legacy for land. Another way to honor land is to share the written or oral history of your farm. You can aim to accomplish the need for land to have a legacy through stories, songs, poems, and many other creative art forms.

References

"A 50-Year Farm Bill." *The Land Institute*, 2009, www.landinstitute.org.

Berry, Wendell. *Our Only World*. 2015. Counterpoint.

Ehl, Dan. "Aronia Berries—Good for Health, the Land and Smaller Farms." *The Kalona News*, Section C, March 27, 2014.

Einstein, Albert. *Legendary Quotes*, www.legendary-quotes.website. Accessed January 2020.

Fullerton, John. *Regenerative Capitalism: How universal principles and patterns will shape our new economy*. April, 2015. Capital Institute.

Harvey, Paul. "So God Made A Farmer." *American Broadcasting Company*, 1986.

Jospe, Christophe. "Do it, prove it, sell it: my evolving views on carbon accounting." www.cjospe.medium.com, Accessed January 2021.

Lombardi, Vince. *Legendary Quotes*, www.legendary-quotes.website, Accessed January 2021.

Lyle, Levi. "Regenerative Stewardship." www.levilyle/blogspot.com Accessed January 2021.

Lyle, Levi. *Ice Sage: Living and Loving the Land Poems*. First World Publishing. 2020.

Lyle, Levi. *Ice Sage: Living and Loving the Land Prose*. First World Publishing. 2022 (forthcoming).

Lyle, Levi. *Legendary Quotes*, www.legendary-quotes.website. Accessed January 2021.

National Agricultural Statistics Service (NASS) 2017, USDA. www.nass.usda.gov

National Agricultural Statistics Service (NASS) 2019, USDA. https://www.nass.usda.gov/Statistics_by_State/Iowa/Publications/Other_Surveys/2020/IA-Certified-Organic-10-20.pdf

Woida, Kathleen. *Iowa's Remarkable Soils: The Story of Our Most Vital Resource and How We Can Save It*. University of Iowa Press. 2021.